HOW TO FOSTER A WORKPLACE CULTURE THAT VALUES MENTAL WELLNESS

For Leaders and Managers Who Want Results

Mike Veny, Inc. is accredited by the International Association for Continuing Education and Training (IACET). Mike Veny, Inc. complies with the ANSI/IACET Standard, which is recognized internationally as a standard of excellence in instructional practices. As a result of this accreditation, Mike Veny, Inc. is accredited to issue the IACET CEU.

Mike Veny, Inc. is also recognized by the Society for Human Resources Management (SHRM) to offer Professional Development Credits (PDCs) for SHRM-CP® or SHRM-SCP®. The company is also a Human Resources Certification Institute (HRCI) Accredited Provider.

DEDICATION

This book is dedicated to the leaders and managers who believe that a mentally healthy work environment is possible. Thank you for investing in the people you serve.

DISCLAIMER

Trigger Warning: This book discusses violence, self-harm, and suicide.

If you or someone you know may be struggling with suicidal thoughts, you can call the **US National Suicide Prevention Lifeline at 800-273-TALK (8255)** anytime, day or night.

Disclaimer: The purpose of this book is to educate. The author and/or publisher shall have neither liability nor responsibility to anyone with respect to any loss or damage caused, directly or indirectly, by the information contained in this book. The author is not a mental health professional. If you need medical help, please consult a doctor. **If you are in an emergency, please call 911.**

Limit of Liability/Disclaimer of Warranty: While the publisher and author have used their best efforts in preparing this book, they make no representations or warranties with respect to the accuracy or completeness of the contents of this book and specifically disclaim any implied warranties of merchantability or fitness for a particular purpose. No warranty may be created or extended by sales representatives or written sales materials. The advice and strategies contained herein may not be suitable for your situation. You should consult with a professional when appropriate. Neither the publisher nor the author shall be liable for damages arising herefrom.

Author Note: Throughout this book, the author uses the terms "mental health challenges," "mental health concerns," and "mental health conditions" in places where one might typically say, "mental health issues" or "mental illness." He made the decision to do this because it feels less stigmatizing to him.

Some names and identifying details have been changed to protect the privacy of individuals.

We hope you find this book to be useful. If you have any feedback or questions, here's how to contact the author:

Mike Veny
Mobile: +1 (213) 458-8369
Email: mike@mikeveny.com
www.mikeveny.com

ENDORSEMENTS

"This was such a great presentation. Your presentation style is so engaging and accepting, and your story is one that inspires hope with those struggling with mental health challenges."

—Employee
MICROSOFT

"Had the privilege and honor to listen to Mike Veny sharing his wisdom and experience concerning mental health. Mike, you are such a beacon of light for so many suffering in silence."

—Employee
T-MOBILE

"It's remarkable we have these kinds of talks, webinars, and resources at Salesforce. It's very inspiring to know we are supported and encouraged to approach these real challenges and issues."

—Employee
SALESFORCE

"Thank you for helping us set the tone for an important day and leaving the Merck team with an experience we'll always remember."

—*Employee*
MERCK

"Mike, it was an honor for us to be in your company, you had such an impact. Thank you so much for helping us raise awareness of the stigma associated with mental health and how to combat it together."

—*Employee*
HEINEKEN USA

TABLE OF CONTENTS

INTRODUCTION

M ENTAL HEALTH IS AN ISSUE in your workplace. Let me clarify this statement. **Mental health is an issue in every workplace.**

Does your organization provide a safe environment for employees who live with mental health challenges? Unfortunately, according to your employees, the answer is no. A mere 5 percent of employees strongly agree that their employer provides a safe environment for employees who live with a mental illness, according to Mental Health America's (MHA) Mind the Workplace 2021 Report. This means that 95 percent of employees, and the vast majority of your team, believe that their employer needs to do more for employees with mental health challenges.

According to the Centers for Disease Control and Prevention (CDC), nearly one in five adults have a mental health challenge in any given year, and nearly three out of four (71 percent) report at least one symptom of stress (CDC 2018). With the majority of your workforce suffering from stress and mental health challenges, their quality of work and level of satisfaction at work will be impacted. Stress leads to burnout, which directly affects the productivity and energy of an employee, which affects both their work and home life.

Employee burnout, according to a recent Indeed report, is on the rise (Threlkeld 2021). A staggering 52 percent of all workers feel burned out, which is an increase of nearly 10 percent since a similar survey was conducted before the COVID pandemic.

In the United States alone, workplace stress and burnout lead to approximately 120,000 deaths and close to $190B in spending each year (Moss 2019). According to the American Psychological Association (APA), burnout leads to high turnover rates, lower productivity, and increased healthcare costs.

The burden of preventing burnout does not lie on an individual employee, as previously believed, but their employer (Moss 2019). Your organization has a responsibility to support the mental health of employees, for the health of your company and the health of your employees.

Your workplace doesn't have to be mentally unhealthy. Mental health should be a strength in your workplace. Burnout can be prevented, and the mental wellness of your employees can be supported and improved. However, it takes intentional action. To turn mental health from liability to strength through intentional actions, you need the following:

1. To know and understand the benefits of mental health initiatives in the workplace.

2. An understanding of the importance of talking about mental health in the workplace.

3. To understand how to foster a workplace culture that values mental wellness.

4. The ability to identify when an employee is struggling.

5. To know how to have a conversation with employees about their mental health.

In this book, we will cover only the third of these five areas. The others are addressed in Connectivity & Conversations, a self-study, continuing education course to help human resource professionals and managers feel prepared and confident when faced with an employee who may be experiencing a mental health concern.

By implementing this knowledge and these tools in your workplace, you will turn mental health into a strength and empower your employees to be happy, healthy, and productive.

My name is Mike Veny, and I am a Certified Corporate Wellness Specialist®, best-selling author on mental health, and one of the 100 most influential people in the healthcare industry according to PM360 ELITE (2017). My mission is to support you in discovering the gift of emotional wellness through unique learning experiences designed to empower your personal and professional growth.

Throughout my entire life and for the rest of my life, I have and will probably continue to struggle with mental health challenges. I wrote *Transforming Stigma: How to Become A Mental Wellness Superhero* to tell my story and empower others to become what I have strived to be over the last decade—a mental wellness superhero.

Currently, I live with major depressive disorder, anxiety, and obsessive-compulsive disorder, also known as OCD. My mental health challenges, at their worst, really negatively affected my life, especially as a child. I was hospitalized in a mental hospital three times as a kid, expelled from three schools, attempted to die by suicide at age ten, I was violent at home, engaged in self-harm, and was on many medications. As an adult, I still struggle. It has really affected my professional career as a musician. The different band leaders were essentially multiple supervisors, and if my anxiety would come up, I always wondered what would happen if they found out. Would they want to fire me, or would word spread that something is a little "off" about me?

I have used these challenges to fuel my life's work— to promote mental wellness. We all have the ability to support and empower those with mental health concerns, but it takes intentional effort, skills, and understanding to become a superhero. Trust me, you do not have to be a Certified Corporate Wellness Specialist®, author, or a person with lived experience to support your employees, but you will benefit from learning from one.

Over the past two years, I have worked with Merck, T-Mobile, Microsoft, CVS Health, Heineken, Ford, Wounded Warrior Project, and more to make mental wellness a priority in their workplaces. These organizations are thinking ahead about their employees in a way that directly impacts their bottom line, and you will be too, when you implement what you learn in this book. You are taking action *before* disaster strikes, as I have seen my past clients do for their employees.

> *"It's very inspiring to know we are*
> *supported and encouraged to approach*
> *these real challenges and issues."*
> —Salesforce employee

> *"Mike, you are such a beacon of light*
> *for so many suffering in silence."*
> —Melanie Kiely, T-Mobile

> *"Thank you so much for helping us raise*
> *awareness of the stigma associated with mental*
> *health & how to combat it, together."*
> —Cat Kennedy, Heineken USA

This book and the time you are taking to read and

implement this information is an investment in your company and employees. *How To Foster A Workplace Culture That Values Mental Wellness* will elevate your corporate culture and empower your employees while decreasing turnover, increasing productivity, and decreasing rising healthcare costs.

If you incorporate the information in this book into your workplace, I can guarantee you that you will witness a measurable increase in the happiness and productivity of your employees. This book will change lives, starting with yours. When you are confident in addressing mental health in your workplace, which you will be after reading this book, employees will begin to see it.

By investing in their mental health, you give them proof that you care about their well-being, and they will pass that care on to their work. I have seen this play out time and time again, and I am excited to hear your success story.

Don't let the 95 percent of employees who believe their employer does not provide a safe environment for employees with mental health challenges statistic be true at your company. Take action today by completing this book and implementing these practices into your corporate culture. While I have worked with employers who have regretted not acting sooner to address the mental health of their employees, I have never met a CEO, entrepreneur, manager, or HR team that has regretted focusing on the mental health of their employees. You can be the spark that ignites change in your organization. Everything you need is in the following five sections.

Your employees and I thank you in advance for taking this journey, and in time, so will your clients, employers, shareholders, and fellow managers. Mental health initiatives have a HUGE ROI (return on investment). Let's begin our journey!

HOW TO FOSTER A WORKPLACE CULTURE THAT VALUES MENTAL WELLNESS

WHAT IS THE STATE OF your workplace culture?

As humans, we have a deep need for a sense of belonging. We bring this need with us into the workplace. Making genuine connections with employees and empowering them to connect with each other is critical for building an inclusive workplace because if you don't have an inclusive workplace, you will have employees who feel as though they don't belong there.

In order to gain clarity and truly understand what it's like to build an inclusive workplace, take a few minutes to complete the workplace self-assessment below. Continue on to the reflection portion of the assessment, which will help you create and record your ideas for improving workplace culture and supporting employees' mental wellness.

WORKPLACE CULTURE ASSESSMENT

NOTE: This assessment is meant to help you understand needs for improvement in your organization and your own personal leadership style. It is not a scientific assessment.

Part 1: Organizational Assessment

x	Description
	The organization has clearly defined core values that focus on human qualities rather than only the bottom line. (For example, "Integrity" is human-focused, while "Efficiency" is company-focused.)
	The organization's top leaders model ethical, caring, and supportive behavior.
	An Employee Assistance Program is available to all employees.
	Expectations for employees are reasonable and clearly communicated.
	Most employees stay with the organization longer than five years.
	Communication occurs freely at all levels (top-down, bottom-up, cross-functionally).
	Employees receive timely information they need to perform their jobs.
	Ample leave time is provided (e.g., sick days, personal days, holidays, etc.).
	Employees are recognized for a job well done.
	Organizational leadership reflects the diversity of the employees.
	Mentoring or coaching is available to employees.
	Employees are likely to go to lunch or enjoy other social gatherings together.
	TOTAL

Add up your checkboxes to find out how mentally well your workplace is.

- **10–12:** Looking great! Your organization seems to truly care about its employees.
- **8–9:** Not bad, but the organization can do better.
- **5–7:** Employees will need strong support to be successful in this stressful environment.
- **1–4:** Why are you still there? Get out while you still can!

Part 2: Self-Assessment

Reflect on each statement. Write the number of your answer in each blank.

Description	Rarely (1)	Sometimes (2)	Usually (3)	Always (4)
I actively seek ways to make connections with my employees.				
I ask for input from team members on matters affecting the team.				
I make sure employees' individual contributions are recognized.				
I know each employee well (e.g., hobbies, personal interests, family).				
I empower employees to make decisions about their work.				

Description	Rarely (1)	Sometimes (2)	Usually (3)	Always (4)
I show genuine concern for my employees' well-being.				
I set a positive example for employees by practicing good work-life balance.				
I value the differences on my team.				
My employees know I value them as people.				
I listen carefully when my employees talk to me.				
I seek feedback from my employees.				
I communicate effectively with my team.				
I make sure everyone is heard.				
TOTALS:				

Add up your totals across all columns to see how you did:

- **40–52:** You are clearly a caring leader who values your team members. Keep it up!
- **27–39:** You're definitely making an effort to

connect with your employees, but there's still room for improvement. Make time every day to check in with your team and show them you care.

- **<26:** Maybe you are so focused on getting the work done that you aren't making time for connecting with your employees. Remember, we're all only human. Make some time to form relationships with your team members and show them you care. You'll be amazed at the results!

Part Three: Reflection

Now that you have a better understanding of how your organizational culture and your own leadership style affect your employees' mental wellness, take a few moments to reflect on the results. Write down some specific things you will commit to doing that will improve the mental wellness culture in your workplace:

Ideas for Making Connections and Communicating with Employees

____

____

____

____

____

____

____

Ideas for Getting Input and Feedback from Employees

MIKE VENY

Ideas for Improving Work-Life Balance

MIKE VENY

Other Ideas for Improving Workplace Culture

CULTIVATE BELONGING AND PROMOTE WELLNESS

TO CREATE A MENTALLY HEALTHY workplace culture, leaders must be intentional about making a genuine connection with each employee. Establishing genuine connections may seem challenging and time-intensive, but creating these connections can be as simple as being fully present during conversations and meetings. As Stephen R. Covey, author of *The 7 Habits of Highly Effective People*, says, "Most people do not listen with the intent to understand; they listen with the intent to reply." When someone is talking, we are all guilty of being occupied with what we'll say in response instead of hearing them and showing them that we are listening.

When we aren't aware that we are focusing on our response rather than listening, it becomes a barrier to supporting the mental wellness of employees. The barrier forms because when you listen in order to *respond*, you're shifting the conversation to be about yourself. Instead, strive to get in the habit of listening to *understand*. Really hear what your employee is telling you and wait to think about your response until you have fully listened and processed what they have said to you.

So, some tips on listening. It's extremely important to be present when you're listening to someone. You need to constantly strive to put yourself in the other person's shoes. That means putting your own stuff aside and just stepping into their mind, looking at the world through their eyes. That effort can be felt by the other person and creates connection.

Another helpful thing to do is ask clarifying questions. "So just so I'm clear…," "Just so I understand…," "I want to make sure I'm understanding what you're saying." Saying things like that is important.

When you listen to understand, not only will you be able to support an employee when they are struggling, but you will also build trust in your relationships and increase your influence as a leader. Also, when someone tells you that something is wrong, trust your intuition and don't be afraid to ask people how they're doing. Give them a chance to express themselves and share in a safe environment. Employee mental wellness aside, these practices will support you in being a successful supervisor, manager, leader, and overall human being.

Are you willing to commit to making a real effort to get to know your employees? If you believe you already know your employees, I encourage you to make a new commitment to learn *more* about them and deepen existing relationships.

The stronger your connections are with employees, the more comfortable they will be with you, the company, their work, and their fellow employees. And most importantly, the more you know about each of your employees, the more likely you are to UNDERSTAND and KNOW when they are struggling.

At the same time, it's important to maintain professional boundaries with your employees. It's a difficult balance to strike, but it's not impossible and truly worth the investment.

CONCLUSION

W ELL, WE'VE COME TO THE end of our journey together. I hope that you have found this material useful for making lasting change in your organization. It's important that you're intentional about communicating your commitment to mental wellness to the people that you serve. Using this book as a tool to start making permanent changes in your culture is one of the first steps that you can take toward building trust and improving the wellness of your work community. Being open and clear in letting people know what steps they can take if they want to discuss mental health or need resources is essential.

I hope this material got you thinking. I would love to say it's complete, but there are always things that are missing and can be improved. And as time goes on, I will do my best to add them as I see fit, so we can make this a better resource.

As someone who has struggled for his entire life with mental health challenges, I want to say thank you for taking the time to read this book. Thank you for putting your energy into this work. And most importantly, thank you for your trust.

If you have enjoyed and gained value from this book, could you take a minute to leave a review on Amazon? Your review will help others find this book. Thank you in advance for furthering the conversation on workplace wellness!

APPENDIX 1: MENTAL HEALTH HOTLINES & WEBSITES

THE FOLLOWING IS A LIST of resources that could help you to either get the help you need or the information you are looking for. However, I have not personally used every one of these resources and am not personally endorsing any of them. It's up to you to determine if they can benefit you, but if you are struggling, I urge you to reach out to one of these resources.

CRISIS / SUICIDE PREVENTION

The National Suicide Prevention Lifeline

The National Suicide Prevention Lifeline is a free service that can be used by anyone who is experiencing suicidal thoughts, family members who are concerned about a loved one, and professionals who are looking for additional resources. You can speak with someone over the phone and they can put you in contact with a local center. This is available 24/7 so someone will be there whenever you need them.

Phone: 1-800-273-TALK (8255)
Website: http://suicidepreventionlifeline.org

The American Foundation for Suicide Prevention

The American Foundation for Suicide Prevention works to fund scientific research and raise awareness for those that are struggling with or affected by suicide. They provide resources for support groups and professionals as well as to individuals struggling with suicidal thinking.

Phone: 1-888-333-2377
Website: https://afsp.org

HopeLine

Hopeline is an organization that's made up of independent volunteers. It's a confidential telephone service for people who are in crisis. Their volunteers are not professional counselors. If they feel that your situation is outside of what they are able to assist with, they will connect you to the appropriate referral.

Phone: 1-877-235-4525 (call or text)
Website: https://www.hopeline-nc.org

Crisis Text Line

Crisis Text Line is a free hotline that has counselors available 24/7 to help anyone in crisis. If you aren't comfortable talking to someone, texting can be a good option for getting the help you need.

Text the word CONNECT to 741741

IMALIVE

IMALIVE is an online chat based resource. It's run by the Kristin Brooks Hope Center. They run programs for high schools and colleges along with having the online crisis chat. If you are experiencing a crisis, have suicidal thoughts, or are dealing with intense emotional pain, the volunteers on their chatline can help.

Website: https://www.imalive.org

GAMBLING

National Council on Problem Gambling
The National Council on Problem Gambling offers several ways that those addicted to gambling and their families can get help. They provide literature on treatment and recovery options and the hotline can help you get connected with local resources.

Phone: 1-800-522-4700
Chat: www.ncpagambling.org/chat
Online peer support forum: www.gamtalk.org
Website: https://www.ncpagambling.org

GRIEF

Compassionate Friends
Compassionate Friends provides help for family

members after the death of a child. They offer support through local chapters and online communities. There is a wealth of knowledge on their website and you can request a Bereavement Packet that can be customized to your situation. Through their website, you can find the closest chapter to you from their list of over 600 chapters.

Phone: 1-630-990-0010
Website: https://www.compassionatefriends.org

LGBTQ SUPPORT

LGBT National Hotline
The LGBT National Help Center works to assist people who have questions about gender identity and sexual orientation. They run three hotlines and offer private one-on-one chat online. They can help with issues like coming-out, safer sex, school bullying, relationship problems, and family concerns. They also have online chat rooms for youth and teens to help them find a community of acceptance.

Phone: 1-888-843-4564
LGBT National Youth Talkline: 1-800-246-7743
LGBT National Senior Talkline: 1-888-234-7243
Email: help@LGBThotline.org
Website: https://www.glbthotline.org

MENTAL HEALTH

National Alliance on Mental Illness (NAMI)

NAMI does not provide counseling, however they do provide information about mental health issues such as symptoms and treatment options. They can also help connect you with support groups. You can reach out to the national office to be connected with your state chapter or you can find out more information on their website.

Phone: 1-800-950-6264
Website: http://www.nami.org

Anxiety and Depression Association of America (ADAA)

The ADAA provides access to information to help in the prevention and treatment of anxiety and depression. Their website is full of information and they do have an option to find a local therapist.

Phone: 1-240-485-1001
Website: https://adaa.org

Children and Adults with Attention Deficit Hyperactivity Disorder CHADD)

The CHADD's website has information for professionals, educators, parents, and adults who are living with ADHD. You can reach a specialist on the phone from 1:00 p.m. to 5:00 p.m. EST Monday through Friday.

Phone:1- 800-233-4050
Website: https://chadd.org

International OCD Foundation

The International OCD Foundation has resources and information to help you learn more about OCD. They can also help connect you with trained professionals within your local area.

Phone: 1-617-973-5801
Website: https://iocdf.org

Treatment and Research Advancements for Borderline Personality Disorder (TARA)

TARA provides access to researched-based information and help to cope with Borderline Personality Disorder. Whether you are the one struggling or it's one of your loved ones, they can connect you with local resources that offer treatment and support.

Phone: 1-888-482-7227
Website: www.tara4bpd.org

SUBSTANCE ABUSE

Substance Abuse and Mental Health Services Administration (SAMHSA)

SAMHSA's mission is to "reduce the impact of substance abuse and mental illness on America's communities". This agency is part of the U.S. Department of Health and Human Services. They provide information that can help you locate treatment options within your area. The office is open Monday through Friday from 8 a.m. to 8 p.m. EST.

Phone: 1-877-SAMHSA7 (1-877-726-4727)
Website: https://www.samhsa.gov

National Council on Alcoholism and Drug Dependence (NCADD)
NCADD works to connect individuals to the right resources in their community to help them recover from addiction. When you call the number below you will be redirected to a local center based on the zip code you enter.

Phone: 1-800-622-2255
Website: https://www.ncadd.org

Partnership for Drug-Free Kids

This free hotline provides one-on-one help for parents, family members, or caregivers who are looking for help with a child's substance abuse. The phones are answered by trained specialists Monday through Friday from 9 a.m. to midnight EST and Saturday & Sunday from 12:00 p.m. through 5 p.m. EST.

Phone: 1-855-378-4373
Text: 55753
Website: https://drugfree.org (you can also email a specialist from a form on the website)

Trevor HelpLine

The Trevor Project works to provide suicide intervention and crisis intervention for LGBTQ individuals that are under the age of 25. The hotline is available 24/7, the online chat and text option is available every day from Noon through 1 a.m. EST.

Phone: 1-866-488-7386
Text the word START to 678678
Website: https://www.thetrevorproject.org

Teen Line

Teen Line provides teen-to-teen support from 9:00 p.m. to 1:00 a.m. EST for teenagers who are struggling and want to talk to another teen who knows what they're talking about. They also provide resources, information, and offer message boards.

Phone: 1-800-852-8336
Text the word TEEN to 839863

VETERANS

Veterans Crisis Line
The Veterans Crisis Line is there 24/7 to support any veterans, service members, National Guard and the Reserve, or their family and friends who are experiencing a crisis. There are qualified responders from the Department of Veterans Affairs that you can contact by calling, texting, or using an online chat.

Phone: 1-800-273-8255
Text: 838255
Chat: connect on their website https://www. veteranscrisisline.net

APPENDIX 2: HOW TO USE A MENTAL HEALTH HOTLINE

IF YOU OR A LOVED one is struggling with mental health, know that you are not alone. You are not the only person to feel like you do, and there are people who care about you and want to help. If you don't know who to turn to, there are plenty of hotlines that you can call. The people who answer these calls are there because you are important and they want to assist you in getting help.

If you think there is any chance that you or someone else you know might harm yourself or others, contact 911 immediately.

But if you simply don't know where to turn to get help for yourself or someone else, or if you don't know if you even should call someone, I urge you to reach out to one of the numbers below.

WHO SHOULD CALL

Anyone can call a mental health hotline. The people on the other end of the phone are trained to speak to people suffering from mental health challenges, family members who are at a loss of knowing what to do next, and people who just have questions in general.

Do not feel that your situation is not "bad enough" or a "big enough deal" to warrant calling a hotline. These hotlines are here to serve people whether you have a simple question or need to find professional help.

WHAT TO EXPECT FROM YOUR CALL

I know that it can be intimidating and maybe even a little scary to pick up a phone and make the call. But there's no reason to be afraid. While each hotline is slightly different, here is what you can generally expect from the experience.

- When the phone is answered you will hear a recorded message. It may include things like what button to push based on your language.

- The recording will tell you if you're going to be routed to a local center and then you will hold while someone is placed on your call.

- A trained counselor will answer your call. Many hotlines don't require you to provide your name if you aren't comfortable doing so.

- The call is entirely about you and to help you. The counselor may ask you some questions about your situation if you are having a difficult time communicating why you called. They will listen to you. They will also provide resources that will be beneficial based on your situation.

Remember, you are in complete control of the call. The person is simply there to help you. They can be a listening ear, connect you with a mental health professional, or provide you with options of next steps that you could take. The calls are confidential unless you specify that you would like them to share the information or if they believe that you are a danger to yourself or someone else.

APPENDIX 3: MENTAL HEALTH MYTHS VS. FACTS

THERE ARE A LOT OF myths that surround mental health. These myths are a large part of what builds the stigma that surrounds mental health challenges. Believing these myths is what's behind the actions that people take and the way they treat and think about those with mental health challenges. But that's not all. There are many people struggling with their own mental health who believe these myths. That's part of what keeps them unable to move forward toward recovery.

I encourage you to read through this next section with an open mind. Use the information and links provided to challenge and change the myths that you've been believing:

MYTH: PEOPLE DIAGNOSED WITH MENTAL HEALTH DISORDERS ARE MORE DANGEROUS.

This myth is commonly found in the media, especially after tragic events like mass shootings. The common belief is that people with mental illness, especially diagnoses such as schizophrenia and bipolar disorder, are more likely to commit a crime.

Fact: People diagnosed with mental illness are actually more likely to be the victim of a crime than to commit a crime themselves. When there are tragic events such as mass shootings, people are quick to throw mental health into the conversation. However, the American Mental Health Counselors Association has stated that including incidents with firearms, mental health is behind only 3 to 5 percent of all violent crimes.

Source for more information:
http://www.mentalhealthamerica.net/positions/violence and http://www.amhca.org

Tip: Share your story! If more people who struggle with mental health were willing to share their stories, society would become familiar with the truth about mental health challenges. If you struggle yourself, don't be afraid to share your experience with others. It will help everyone in the end.

MYTH: PEOPLE WITH MENTAL HEALTH CHALLENGES AREN'T ABLE TO FUNCTION IN SOCIETY.

Fact: One in four people will be impacted by a mental health challenge at some point in their life. There are many levels of mental health challenges, from anxiety and depression to schizophrenia and psychosis. The truth is, you are crossing paths and interacting with people every day who are "mentally ill", you just don't realize it. While there are some instances where those struggling with mental health challenges are unable to function in society on their own, that's the exception and not the rule.

Source for more information: https://www.who.int/whr/2001/media_centre/press_release/en/

Tip: If you are struggling with your mental health to the point that you are struggling to function in your daily life, then you need to seek professional help. There are many forms of treatment for mental health and there's a good chance that finding the right combination of treatment options will help restore your daily life function.

MYTH: MENTAL HEALTH IS NOT A PROBLEM FOR CHILDREN.

Fact: Adults aren't the only ones who experience mental health challenges. One in five children will suffer from challenges with their mental health. This myth is incredibly dangerous to the mental health of children because there are many statistics showing that early detection is a very important part of recovery. The sooner the child is treated, the less likely their chance of developing serious problems with their mental health. However, only a third of children are receiving the treatment they need at this time.

Source for more information:
http://www.mentalhealthamerica.net/ positions/early-identification

Tip: If you have a child who seems like they could be struggling, do not delay in taking them to see a professional. If they get the help they need now, it could stop them from experiencing further challenges in the future.

MYTH: IF SOMEONE WANTS TO STOP STRUGGLING WITH THEIR MENTAL HEALTH, ALL THEY HAVE TO DO IS CHOOSE TO STOP.

Fact: Mental health challenges are real health conditions. They can be caused by genetics, brain chemistry, and exposure to environmental stressors prior to birth. Just because you can't physically see what other people are experiencing does not mean it's not real. People are not choosing to have it in their life. For example, someone who is diagnosed with depression can't simply decide that they are going to "feel better" and "be happy". This can be difficult for people to understand if they haven't experienced it themselves.

Source for more information:
http://www.mentalhealthamerica.net/
recognizing-warning-signs and https://
www.mayoclinic.org/diseases-conditions/
mental-illness/symptoms-causes/syc-20374968

Tip: If you've never experienced mental health challenges personally, you're doing the right thing by reading this book. Continue to educate yourself on the topic to increase your understanding and don't pass judgment onto those who are struggling. Ask them to explain their experience to you.

If you have mental health challenges and are being judged by others, stand up for yourself. Some people won't understand no matter how hard you try to educate them. When that happens you might need to distance yourself from them if they continue to give you a hard time. Talk to a therapist for support.

MYTH: THERE'S NO REAL RECOVERY FROM MENTAL HEALTH CHALLENGES. ONCE YOU HAVE IT, YOU HAVE TO DEAL WITH IT FOR LIFE.

Fact: Mental health challenges are treatable. There are also instances where people only experience symptoms from a mental health challenge for a brief period of time in their life. Just because someone has received a diagnosis does not necessarily mean it's something that they will always deal with. And there are many forms of treatment available to help individuals work toward recovery while improving their quality of life.

Source for more information:
http://www.mentalhealthamerica.
net/recovery-support

Tip: If you are struggling with your mental health, don't lose hope. There are many options available for treatment based on the specific challenges you are facing. Make an appointment and get help from a licensed mental health professional. With trial and error, you will be able to discover a treatment plan that works for you.

MYTH: MEDICATION IS THE ONLY FORM OF TREATMENT.

Fact: There are many different options for treatment. Licensed therapists have a vast number of types of therapies that they can use when treating you. There are also options such as support groups, psychiatric service dogs, meditation, self-care, and more. For some people, medication will be a part of the treatment plan that works for them. However, there are some people who will be able to create a treatment plan without the need for a prescription.

Source for more information:
https://www.psychiatry.org/patients-families/what-is-mental-illness and http://www.mentalhealthamerica.net/types-mental-health-treatments

Tip: If you are treating your mental health challenges only with medication, I encourage you to try including other forms of therapy as well. It could allow you to reduce the medication you are taking or eliminate it altogether. However, there is no shame in using medication to help you with your mental health challenges. Find the program that works best for you.

MYTH: THERE'S NOTHING I CAN DO TO HELP SOMEONE WITH MENTAL HEALTH CHALLENGES.

Fact: Many people believe that because they are not professionals, there's nothing they can do to help those with mental health challenges. And it might be true that you can provide them with therapy, but the truth is, that's not what they need from you. Hurting and struggling people need support. They need to know that they aren't being judged and that there are people for them. They may not even reach out to talk to you about it, but just knowing that you are there if they want to can make all the difference.

Source for more information: You're holding it in your hands right now.

Tip: Look back through this book and pick one actionable thing to do. If you know someone who is struggling, reach out to them. If you don't personally know of anyone, then look for ways to fight the stigma in your community.

APPENDIX 4: SUGGESTED READING LIST

THE DEPRESSION CURE: THE 6-STEP PROGRAM TO BEAT DEPRESSION WITHOUT DRUGS

IN THIS BOOK, AUTHOR STEPHEN Ilardi shares a six-step program based on his proven Therapeutic Lifestyle Change program. He theorizes that we are seeing such high levels of depression in society today because our bodies were not designed to handle the current way that most of us live. His six steps take you back to the way people used to survive and the way some cultures, like aboriginal groups, still do. This includes the following components:

- Brain Food

- Don't Think, Do

- Antidepressant Exercise

- Let There Be Light

- Get Connected

- Habits of Healthy Sleep

If you are looking for alternative or supplemental treatment ideas for depression, this book is for you.

THE BODY KEEPS THE SCORE: BRAIN, MIND, AND BODY IN THE HEALING OF TRAUMA

In this book, author Dr. Bessel van der Kolk explains the physical impact that trauma (all forms, like physical, sexual, and emotional abuse) has on our brain.

Dr. van der Kolk explains that trauma can actually rewire the way our brain works. This makes an impact on our levels of control, engagement, trust, and pleasure. He also shares what we can do that will help us undo the damage including mindfulness, yoga, and other therapies.

ANY BOOKS BY STEPHEN HINSHAW

Stephen Hinshaw has written multiple books that are helpful resources on mental health. He has a long list of accomplishments in the field of mental health, including being a professor of psychology at both UC San Francisco and UC Berkeley and has been recognized by groups across the country.

ADHD: What Everyone Needs to Know

The Mark of Shame: Signs of Mental Illness and Agenda for Change

Breaking the Silence: Mental Health Professionals Disclose Their Personal and Family Experiences with Mental Illness

The Triple Bind: Saving Our Teenage Girls from Today's Pressures and Conflicting Expectations

Origins of the Human Mind

The ADHD Explosion: Myths, Medication, Money, and Today's Push for Performance

Another Kind of Madness: A Journey Through the Stigma and Hope of Mental Illness

ANY BOOKS BY PATRICK CORRIGAN

Patrick Corrigan is a professor of psychology at the Illinois Institute of Technology. He has held many other prestigious positions and has devoted decades to helping patients with psychiatric disabilities and their families. This past decade he has largely focused on addressing the stigma surrounding mental health.

Challenging the Stigma of Mental Illness: Lessons for Therapists and Advocates (written with David Roe and Hector W. H. Tsang)

Don't Call Me Nuts: Coping with the Stigma of Mental Illness (written with Robert Lundin)

The Stigma of Disease and Disability: Understanding Causes and Overcoming Injustices

Coming Out Proud to Erase the Stigma of Mental Illness: Stories and Essays of Solidarity (written with Jon E. Larson and Patrick J. Michaels)

Recovery in Mental Illness: Broadening Our Understanding of Wellness (written with Ruth O. Ralph)

I HATE YOU—DON'T LEAVE ME: UNDERSTANDING THE BORDERLINE PERSONALITY

For more than two decades, this book by Jerold Kreisman has been considered the guide to BPD. It dives into the disorder along with its connection to other mental health disorders. There is a revised and updated book on the market. If you are looking to understand your BPD or just want a better understanding of the disorder, this is a great book to check out.

ANXIETY SUCKS! A TEEN SURVIVAL GUIDE

This book by Natasha Daniels is a great read for teens

and adults. It breaks down what anxiety looks and sounds like in our lives, providing practical examples that preteens and teens can relate to and easy-to-follow steps they can take in order to overcome it.

CHANGE YOUR BRAIN, CHANGE YOUR LIFE: THE BREAKTHROUGH PROGRAM FOR CONQUERING ANXIETY, DEPRESSION, OBSESSIVENESS, ANGER, AND IMPULSIVENESS

In this book, author Daniel Amen goes into detail about how your brain works and what you can do to pinpoint your problems along with what you can do in order to address each area and improve functionality. It includes options like nutrition, medication, and cognitive exercises. If you are easily controlled by your emotions and experience anxiety and depression, this is a good read.

ACKNOWLEDGMENTS

THE COMPLETION OF THIS PROJECT could have not been made possible without the participation, support, and help from a long list of people. I appreciate all of their efforts and am grateful for their contributions.

However, I would like to express sincere appreciation and indebtedness mainly to the following:

Lacy Anderson for coaching me, giving me guidance on the product development process and most importantly, teaching me to see my business as a product in and of itself.

Ameerah Palacios for pushing me to step out of my comfort zone, along with the art of being intentionally strategic and aggressive simultaneously.

Stephanie Kirby for challenging me to see different perspectives, take risks and live with integrity.

Kayleen Holt for designing this learning experience and inspiring me to enjoy the process of developing a learning experience.

Laura Kaiser for bringing her standard of excellence to this and inspiring me to go the extra mile in making this material useful to the reader.

Christie Stratos for bringing her whole self to putting the final touches on the text and doing it with so much love.

I place on record my sincerest thanks to Michael Luchies. His willingness to jump on another wild adventure with me is what got this book done. But most importantly, I appreciate our mutual love for the movie *Jackie Brown* and the fact that we both truly value the idea of owning a recording by The Delfonics on vinyl.

And last but not least, I'd like to thank my wife, Denelle, for her unconditional love and support. None of this would have been possible without her at my side.

AUTHOR'S NOTE

This is all about mental health in the workplace.

So, if you like *The ROI Of Mental Wellness In The Workplace*, please talk about it! And if you do so online, tag @mikeveny or use the hashtag #mikeveny.

Also, remember that there are many additional resources about mental health in the workplace that didn't fit in the book. Go to www.mikeveny.com to access videos, courses, live events, and special surprises.

SPECIALIZED CONSULTING
FOR YOUR ORGANIZATION

I also work directly with companies to help them create mentally healthy workplaces. If you're intrigued by the premise of a mentally healthy workplace but would like some help making it work in your organization, send me a note at mike@mikeveny.com and I will be in touch immediately.

CONNECTIVITY &
CONVERSATIONS ON STAGE

I also travel the world spreading the message about the importance of human resource professionals and managers feeling prepared and confident when faced with an employee who may be experiencing a mental health concern. I'd be honored to collaborate with you on a keynote, customized workshop, webinar, or other live training opportunity. Just email me at the address above.

ABOUT THE AUTHOR

Mike Veny loves working with leaders who are tired of bringing the same old textbook presentations on mental health or diversity and inclusion to their events. If you are looking for a compelling speaker who will connect with, entertain, and engage your audience—all while educating and uniting them around improving wellness—you've come to the right place.

As a Certified Corporate Wellness Specialist®, Mike's presentations move past simply educating an audience to providing them with actionable steps they can take to change their lives and work environments. His reputation as a dynamic speaker provides confidence and peace of mind for meeting planners everywhere.

The mission of his company, Mike Veny, Inc., is to support you in receiving the gift of emotional wellness through unique learning experiences designed to empower your personal and professional growth. The International Association for Continuing Education and Training has awarded his company the prestigious Accredited Provider accreditation for its continuing education programs.

MIKE'S STORY

Mike's path to becoming a speaker became evident at an early age. He convinced the staff at psychiatric hospitals to discharge him three times during his childhood. In addition to being hospitalized as a child, he was expelled from three schools, attempted suicide, and was medicated in efforts to reduce his emotional instability and behavioral outbursts.

By the fifth grade, Mike was put in a special education class. Aside from getting more individualized attention from the teacher, he learned that pencil erasers make great sounds when tapped on a desk. *He had no idea that drumming would become his career or his path to recovery.*

As an adult, Mike spent many years facilitating drum

workshops for children with special needs, teaching them to channel their energy by banging a drum while also learning how to listen, focus, work together and succeed through teamwork. The project was such a hit that he continued to expand his drumming program, first to adults in recovery and eventually into the corporate setting.

A FEW THINGS YOU MAY FIND OF INTEREST

- His bestselling book *Transforming Stigma: How to Become a Mental Wellness Superhero* and *The Transforming Stigma Workbook* have become valuable mental health resources for people of all ages.

- As a 2017 PM360 ELITE Award Winner, he is recognized as one of the 100 most influential people in the healthcare industry for his work as a patient advocate.

- He has presented for audiences in the corporate world, healthcare systems, K-12 education, professional development for teachers, colleges, and universities.

- He has delivered keynote presentations for Heineken, T-Mobile, Aetna, Salesforce, Sanofi, and CVS Health.

- He is proud to be a member of the Society for Human Resources Management (SHRM), National Diversity Council, Meeting Professionals International, the National Speakers Association and the Rotary Club of Wall Street New York.

- Mike's mission is to help others receive the gift of emotional wellness.

- His presentations can be customized to fit the needs of your event and deliver the results you're looking for.

If you're looking for an easy-to-work-with speaker who transforms a genuine and actionable message into a fun and unforgettable experience, Mike Veny is your choice.

Visit Mike online at www.mikeveny.com.

CONTINUE YOUR JOURNEY OF MENTAL WELLNESS

IGNITE MINI COURSE

The world now has heightened awareness around the responsibility that employers have to help employees manage their mental health and emotional wellness. And Human Resource leaders are tasked with the job of figuring out how to make it happen. The IGNITE Mini Course is a simple way to provide your employees with actionable steps they can use to create a self-care routine in their life.

THE ULTIMATE GUIDE TO SELF-CARE

Employee mental health is one of the most talked-about topics among Human Resource leaders. Recent research shows that approximately 40 percent of employees are struggling with their mental health since the pandemic began (Lyra 2020). The Ultimate Guide to Self-Care gives employees actionable steps to help their mental and emotional wellness.

THE 30-DAY SELF-CARE PLAN

Are you ready for 4 weeks of outstanding wellness? Refresh, renew and recharge your mental and emotional health with The 30-Day Self-Care Plan.

www.mikeveny.com/store

JOIN THE CONVERSATION

My favorite part of teaching is participating in the great conversations that happen on my social media and in my comments section.

Mike's YouTube: http://youtube.com/mikeveny

Mike on LinkedIn: http://linkedin.com/in/mikeveny

Mike on Twitter: @MikeVeny

Mike on Instagram: @MikeVeny

Mike on Facebook: http://facebook.com/mikeveny

REFERENCES

Centers for Disease Control and Prevention. 2018. "Mental Health in the Workplace: Mental Health Disorders and Stress Affect Working-Age Americans." https://www.cdc.gov/workplacehealthpromotion/tools-resources/workplace-health/mental-health/index.html

Kotter. 2011. "Does corporate culture drive financial performance?" Forbes. https://www.forbes.com/sites/johnkotter/2011/02/10/does-corporate-culture-drive-financial-performance/

Mental Health America. n.d. "Workplace Mental Health: Data, Statistics, And Solutions." Accessed September 22, 2021. https://mhanational.org/mind-workplace.

Moss, Jennifer. 2019. "Burnout Is About Your Workplace, Not Your People." Harvard Business Review. https://hbr.org/2019/12/burnout-is-about-your-workplace-not-your-people.

Sapien Labs. 2020. "The Cost of Poor Workplace Mental Health." https://sapienlabs.org/mentalog/the-cost-of-poor-mental-health-in-the-workplace/

Wellness Council of America. 2021. "2021 Workplace Resilience Survey Report." https://www.welcoa.org/resources/2021-workplace-resilience-survey-report/

World Health Organization. 2004. *Promoting mental health: concepts, emerging evidence, practice (Summary Report)* Geneva: World Health Organization.

THANK YOU FOR READING!

Finally, I need to ask a favor. If you're so inclined, I'd LOVE it if you would post a review of this book. Loved it, hated it—I'd just like to hear your feedback. Reviews can be tough to come by these days, and you, the reader, have the power to make or break a book. If you have the time, here's a link to my author page, along with all my books on Amazon: https://amzn.to/3AiFlMJ

Thank you for reading this.

Thank you for spending time with me.

Thank you for your trust.

Mike Veny